THE PRINCESS AND THE JEWEL DOCTOR

Robert Hichens

[ZHINGOORA BOOKS]

This edition is published by
Zhingoora Books.

In St. Petersburg society there may be met at the present time a certain Russian Princess, who is noted for her beauty, for an ugly defect—she has lost the forefinger of her left hand—and for her extraordinary attachment to the city of Tunis, where she has spent at least three months of each year since 1890— the year in which she suffered the accident that deprived her of a finger. What that accident was, and why she is so passionately attached to Tunis, nobody in Russia seems to know, not even her doting husband, who bows to all her caprices. But two persons could explain the matter—a Tunisian guide named Abdul, and a rather mysterious individual who follows a humble calling in the Rue Ben-Ziad, close to the Tunis bazaars. This latter is the Princess's personal attendant during her yearly visit to Tunis. He accompanies her everywhere, may be seen in the hall of her hotel when she is at home, on the box of her carriage when she drives out, close behind her when she is walking. He is her shadow in Africa. Only when she goes back to Russia does he return to his profession in the Rue Ben-Ziad.

This is the exact history of the accident which befell the Princess in 1890. In the spring of that year she arrived one night at Tunis. She had not long been married to an honourable man whom she adored. She was rich, pretty, and popular. Yet her life was clouded by a great fear that sometimes made the darkness of night almost intolerable to her. She dreaded lest the darkness of blindness should come upon her. Both her mother, now dead, and her grandfather had laboured under this defect. They had been born with sight, and had become totally blind ere they reached the age of forty. Princess Danischeff—as we may call her for the purpose of this story—trembled when she thought of their fate, and that it might be hers. Certain books that she read, certain conversations on the subject of heredity that she heard in Petersburg society fed her terror. Occasionally, too, when she stood under a strong light she felt a slight pain in her eyes. She never spoke of her fear, but she fell into a condition of nervous exhaustion that alarmed her husband and her physician. The latter recommended foreign travel as a tonic. The former, who was detained in the capital by political affairs, reluctantly agreed to a separation from his wife. And thus it came about, that, late one night of spring, the Princess and her companion, the elderly Countess de Rosnikoff, arrived in Tunis at the close of a tour in Algeria, and put up at the Hotel Royal.

The bazaars of Tunis are among the best that exist in the world of bazaars, and, on the morning after her arrival, the Princess was anxious to explore them with her companion.

But Madame de Rosnikoff was fatigued by her journey from Constantine. She begged the Princess to go without her, desiring earnestly to be left in her bedroom with a cup of weak tea and a French novel. The Princess, therefore, ordered a guide and set forth to the bazaars.

The guide's name was Abdul. He was a talkative young Eastern, and as he turned with the Princess into the network of tiny alleys that spreads from the Bab-el-bahar to the bazaars, he poured forth a flood of information about the marvels of his native city. The Princess listened idly. That morning she was cruelly pre-occupied. As she stepped out of the hotel into the bright sunshine she had felt a sharp pain in her eyes, and now, though she held over her head a large green parasol, the pain continued. She looked at the light and thought of the darkness that might be coming upon her, and the chatter of Abdul sounded vague in her ears. Presently, however, she was forced to attend to him, for he asked her a direct question.

"To-day they sell jewels by auction near the Mosquée Djama-ez-Zitouna," he said. "Would the gracious Princess like to see the market of the jewels?"

The Princess put her hand to her eyes and assented in a low voice. Abdul turned out of the sunshine into a narrow alley covered with a wooden roof. It was full of shadows and of squatting men, who held out brown hands to the Princess as she passed. But she was staring at the shadows and did not see the merchants of Goblin Market. Leaving this alley Abdul led her abruptly into a dense crowd of Arabs, who were all talking, gesticulating, and moving hither and thither, apparently under the influence of extreme excitement. Many of them held rings, bracelets, or brooches between their fingers, and some extended palms upon which lay quantities of uncut jewels—turquoises, sapphires, and emeralds. At a little distance a grave man was noting down something in a book. But the Princess scarcely observed the progress of the jewel auction. Her attention had been attracted by an extraordinary figure that stood near her. This was an immensely tall Arab, dressed in a dingy brown robe, and wearing upon his shaven head, which narrowed almost to a point at the back, a red fez with a large black tassel. His claw-like hands were covered with rings and his bony wrists with bracelets. But the attention of the Princess was riveted by his eyes. They were small and bright, and squinted horribly—so horribly, that it was impossible to tell at what he was looking. These eyes gave to his face an expression of diabolic and ruthless vigilance and cunning. He seemed at the same time to be seeing everything and to be gazing definitely at nothing.

"That is Safti, the jewel doctor," murmured Abdul in the ear of the Princess.

"A jewel doctor! What is that?" asked the Princess.

"When you are sick he cures you with jewels."

"And what can he cure?" said the Princess, still looking at Safti, who was now bargaining vociferously with a fat Arab for a piece of milk-white jade.

"All things. I was sick of a fever that comes with the summer. He gave me a stone crushed to a powder, and I was well. He saved from death one of the Bey's sons, who was dying from hijada. And then, too, he has a stone in a ring which can preserve sight to him who is going blind."

The Princess started violently.

"Impossible!" she cried.

"It is true," said Abdul. "It is a green stone—like that."

He pointed to an emerald which an Arab was holding up to the light.

The Princess put her hand to her eyes. They still ached, and her temples were throbbing furiously.

"I cannot stay here," she said. "It is too hot. But—— tell the jewel doctor that I wish to visit him. Where does he live?"

"In a little street, Rue Ben-Ziad, in a little house. But he is rich." Abdul spread his arms abroad. "When will the gracious Princess——?"

"This afternoon. At—at four o'clock you will take me."

Abdul spoke to Safti, who turned, squinted horribly at the Princess, and salaamed to her with a curious and contradictory dignity, turning his fingers, covered with jewels, towards the earth.

That afternoon, at four, when the venerable Madame de Rosnikoff was still drinking her weak tea and reading her French novel, the Princess and Abdul stood before the low wooden door of the jewel doctor's house. Abdul struck upon it, and the terrible physician appeared in the dark aperture, looking all ways with his deformed eyes, which fascinated the Princess. Having ascertained that he could speak a little broken French, like many of the Tunisian Arabs, she bade Abdul wait outside, and entered the hovel of the jewel doctor, who shut close the door behind her.

The room in which she found herself was dark and scented. Faint light from the street filtered in through an aperture in the wall, across which was partially drawn a wooden shutter. Round the room ran a divan covered with straw matting, and Safti now conducted the Princess ceremoniously to this, and handed her a cup of thick coffee, which he took from a brass tray that was placed upon a stand. As she sipped the coffee and looked at the pointed head and twisted gaze of Safti, the Princess heard some distant Arab at a street corner singing monotonously a tuneless song, and the scent, the darkness, the reiterated song, and the tall, strange creature standing silently before her gave to her, in their combination, the atmosphere of a dream. She found it difficult to speak, to explain her errand.

At length she said: "You are a doctor? You can cure the sick?"

Safti salaamed.

"With jewels? Is that possible?"

"Jewels are the only medicine," Safti replied, speaking with sudden volubility. "With the ruby I cure madness, with the white jade the disease of the hijada, and with the bloodstone haemorrhage. I have made a man who was ill of fever wear a topaz, and he arose from bed and walked happily in the street."

"And with an emerald," interrupted the Princess; "have you not preserved sight with an emerald? They told me so."

Safti's expression suddenly became grim and suspicious.

"Who said that?" he asked sharply.

"Abdul. Is it true? Can it be true?"

Her cheeks were flushed. She spoke almost with violence, laying her hand upon his arm. Safti seemed to stare hard into the corners of the little room. Perhaps he was really looking at the Princess. At length he said: "It is true."

"I will give any price you ask for it," said the Princess.

"You!" said Safti. "But you—"

Suddenly he lifted his lean hands, took the face of the Princess between them quite gently, and turned it towards the small window. She had begun to tremble. Holding her soft cheeks with his brown fingers, Safti remained motionless for a long time, during which it seemed to the Princess that he was looking away from her at some distant object. She watched his frightful and surreptitious eyes, that never told the truth, she heard the distant Arab's everlasting song, and her dream became a nightmare. At last Safti dropped his hands and said:

"It may be that some day you will need my emerald."

The Princess felt as if at that moment a bullet entered her heart.

"Give it me—give it me!" she cried. "I am rich. I———"

"I do not sell my medicines," Safti answered. "Those who use them must live near me, here in Tunis. When they are healed they give back to me the jewel that has saved them. But you—you live far off."

With the swiftness of a woman the Princess saw that persuasion would be useless. Safti's face looked hard as brown wood. She seemed to recover from her emotion, and said quietly:

"At least you will let me see the emerald?"

Safti went to a small bureau that stood at the back of the room, opened one of its drawers with a key which he drew from beneath his dingy robe, lifted a small silver box carefully out, returned to the Princess, and put the box into her hand.

"Open it," he said.

She obeyed, and took out a very small and antique gold ring, in which was set a rather dull emerald. Safti drew it gently from her, and put it upon the forefinger of her left hand. It was so tiny that it would not pass beyond the joint of the finger, and it looked ugly and odd upon the Princess, who wore many beautiful rings. Now that she saw it she felt the superstition that had sprung from her terror dying within her. Safti, with his crooked eyes, must have read her thought in her face, for he said:

"The Princess is wrong. That medicine could cure her. The one who wears it for three months in each year can never be blind."

Taking the emerald from her finger, he touched her two eyes with it, and it seemed to the Princess that, as he did so, the pain she felt in them withdrew. Her desire for the jewel instantly returned.

"Let me wear it," she said, putting forth all her charm to soften the jewel doctor. "Let me take it with me to Russia. I will make you rich."

Safti shook his head.

"The Princess may wear it here, in Tunis," he replied. "Not elsewhere."

She began to temporise, hoping to conquer his resistance later.

"I may take it with me now?" she asked.

"At a fee."

"I will pay it."

The jewel doctor went to the door, and called in Abdul. Five minutes later the Princess passed the singing Arab at the corner of the street, Rue Ben-Ziad. She had signed a paper pledging herself to return the emerald to Safti at the end of forty-eight hours, and to pay 125 francs for her possession of it during that time. And she wore the emerald on the forefinger of her left hand.

On the following morning Madame de Rosnikoff said to the Princess:

"I hate Tunis. It has an evil climate. The tea here is too strong, and I feel sure the drains are bad. Last night I was feverish. I am always feverish when I am near bad drains."

The Princess, who had slept well, and had waked with no pain in her eyes, answered these complaints cheerily, made the Countess some tea that was really weak, and drove her out in the sunshine to see Carthage. The Countess did not see it, because there is no longer a Carthage. She went to bed that night in a bad humour, and again complained of drains the next morning. This time the Princess did not heed her, for she was thinking of the hour when she must return the emerald to Safti.

"What an ugly ring that is," said the old Countess. "Where did you get it? It is too small. Why do you wear it?"

"I—I bought it in the bazaars," answered the Princess.

"My dear, you wasted your money," said the companion; and she went to bed with another French novel.

That afternoon the Princess implored Safti to sell her the emerald, and as he persistently declined she renewed her lease of it for another forty-eight hours. As she left the jewel doctor's home she did not notice that he spoke some words in a low and eager voice to Abdul, pointing towards her as he did so. Nor did she see the strange bustle of varied life in the street as she walked slowly under the great Moorish arch of the Porte de France. She was deeply thoughtful.

Since she had worn the ugly ring of Safti she had suffered no pain from her eyes, and a strange certainty had gradually come upon her that, while the emerald was in her possession, she would be safe from the terrible disease of which she had so long lived in terror. Yet Safti would not let her have the ring. And she could not live for ever in Tunis. Already she had prolonged her stay abroad, and was due in Russia, where her anxious husband awaited her. She knew not what to do. Suddenly an idea occurred to her. It made her flush red and tingle with shame. She glanced up, and saw the lustrous eyes of Abdul fixed intently upon her. As he left her at the door of the hotel he said,

"The Princess will stay long in Tunis?"

"Another week at least, Abdul," she answered carelessly. "You can go home now. I shall not want you any more to-day."

And she walked into the hotel without looking at him again. When she was in her room she sent for a list of the steamers sailing daily from Tunis for the different ports of Africa and Europe. Presently she came to the bedside of Madame de Rosnikoff.

"Countess," she said, "you are no better?"

"How can I be? The drains are bad, and the tea here is too strong."

"There is a boat that leaves for Sicily at midnight—for Marsala. Shall we go in her?"

The old lady bounded on her pillow.

"Straight on by Italy to Russia?" she cried joyfully.

The Princess nodded. A fierce excitement shone in her pretty eyes, and her little hands were trembling as she looked down at the dull emerald of Safti.

At eleven o'clock that night the Princess and the Countess got into a carriage, drove to the edge of the huge salt lake by which Tunis lies and went on board the Stella d'Italia.

The sky was starless. The winds were still, and it was very dark. As the ship glided out from the shore the old Countess hurried below. But the Princess remained on deck, leaning upon the bulwark, and gazing at the fading lights of the city where Safti dwelt. Two flames seemed burning in her heart, a fierce flame of joy, a fierce flame of contempt—of contempt for herself. For was she not a common thief? She looked at Safti's ring on her finger, and flushed scarlet in the darkness. Yet she was joyful, triumphant, as she heard the beating of the ship's heart, and saw the lights of Tunis growing fainter in the distance, and felt the onward movement of the *Stella d'Italia* through the night. She felt herself nearer to Russia with each throb of the machinery. And from Russia she would expiate her sin. From Russia she would compensate Safti for his loss. The lights of Tunis grew fainter. She thought of the open sea.

But suddenly she felt that the ship was slowing down. The engines beat more feebly, then ceased to beat. The ship glided on for a moment in silence, and stopped. A cold fear ran over the Princess. She called to a sailor.

"Why," she said, "why do we stop? Is anything wrong?"

He pointed to some lights on the port side.

"We are off Hammam-Lif, madame," he said. "We are going to lie to for half-an-hour to take in cargo."

To the Princess that half-hour seemed all eternity. She remained upon deck, and whenever she heard the splash of oars as a boat drew near, or the guttural sound of an Arab voice, she trembled, and, staring into the blackness, fancied that she saw the tall figure, the pointed head, and the deformed eyes of the jewel doctor. But the minutes passed. The cargo was all got on board. The boats drew off. And once again the ship shuddered as the heart of her began to beat, and the ebon water ran backward from her prow.

Then the Princess was glad. She laid the hand on which shone Safti's emerald upon the bulwark, and gazed towards the sea, turning her back upon the lights of Hammam-Lif. She thought of safety, of Russia. She did not hear a soft step drawing near upon the deck behind her. She did not see the flash of steel descending to the bulwark on which her hand was laid.

But suddenly the horrible cry of a woman in agony rang through the night. It was instantly succeeded by a splash in the water, as a tall figure dived over the vessel's side.

When the sun rose on the following day over the minarets of Tunis the *Stella d'Italia*, with the Princess on board, was far out at sea.

The emerald of Safti was once more in the little house in the Rue Ben-Ziad.

It was still upon the Princess's finger.

End of the book.

www.ingramcontent.com/pod-product-compliance
Lightning Source LLC
Chambersburg PA
CBHW071352310526
45790CB00018B/1426

* 9 7 8 1 4 8 4 9 0 5 0 9 8 *